CW01499172

3

4

All you need to know about Cambodia

Introduction

The Southeast Asian region is home to the fascinating country of Cambodia, whose rich history and unique culture have attracted visitors from all over the world for centuries. With an area of about 181,000 square kilometers, Cambodia borders Thailand to the west, Laos to the northwest, Viet Nam to the east, and the Gulf of Thailand to the south. The capital of the country is Phnom Penh, a vibrant metropolis that is also the political, economic and cultural center of the country.

Cambodia's history goes back a long way and is closely linked to the mighty Khmer Empire, which flourished between the 9th and 15th centuries. Under the rule of the Khmer, a complex society developed, characterized by impressive temple buildings such as Angkor Wat, one of the largest religious monuments in the world. These monumental temple complexes remain symbols of the cultural and architectural splendor of ancient Cambodia to this day.

Throughout history, the country has experienced periods of rise and decline, including the period of French colonial rule in the 19th century and the turbulent era of the Khmer Rouge in the 1970s, which left deep wounds in society. After these dark years, Cambodia struggled to rebuild and stability, leading to a period of economic growth and political change that continues to this day.

Cambodia is not only known for its rich history, but also for its impressive nature. From dense rainforests to picturesque rice paddies to the beautiful beaches along the coast, the country offers a variety of landscapes and ecosystems. The wildlife is equally diverse and includes endangered species such as the Indochinese tiger and the Asian elephant.

Cambodian culture is characterized by deep religiosity, especially Theravada Buddhism, which has a significant influence on people's daily lives. Traditional festivals and rituals play an important role in social life, and arts and crafts reflect the country's creative tradition. Cambodian cuisine is known for its variety of flavors and includes dishes such as amok, a delicious curry dish with fish or meat made with coconut milk and spices.

In recent decades, Cambodia has gained increasing popularity as a tourist destination, with visitors attracted not only by the historical sites but also by the hospitality of the locals. The tourism industry has led to an economic boom in many regions of the country, while at the same time efforts are being made to protect cultural heritage and natural resources.

Cambodia's future lies in a balance between modernisation and the preservation of its rich cultural and natural heritage. As the country continues to overcome challenges in the field of sustainable development, it remains a fascinating and inspiring destination for travelers from all over the world who want to discover its beauty and experience its history.

Geography and climate: the land and its natural features

Cambodia, a country of about 181,000 square kilometers, is located in Southeast Asia and shares its borders with Thailand to the west, Laos to the northwest, Viet Nam to the east, and the Gulf of Thailand to the south. The country's geographical diversity ranges from the coastal plain in the south to the central lowlands and the mountainous regions in the northwest. The central lowlands, through which the mighty Mekong River flows, are the agricultural heart of Cambodia and form a fertile base for rice cultivation, which plays a key role in the country's economy.

The landscape of Cambodia is characterized by a mixture of rivers, lakes and tropical rainforests. One of the longest rivers in the world, the Mekong River plays a crucial role in the country's ecological and economic fabric and provides important transport routes for trade. The Tonle Sap, the largest freshwater lake in Southeast Asia, has a unique feature: during the rainy season, water from the Mekong River flows into the lake, significantly increasing its area.

The coastline of Cambodia stretches along the Gulf of Thailand and offers numerous beaches and islands that are increasingly becoming popular destinations. The coastal plain in the south of the country is relatively flat and characterized by mangrove forests, while the central lowlands with their fertile soils extend inland.

To the northwest rises the Dangrek Mountains on the border with Thailand, which is part of the longer Annamite Mountains, which extend to Viet Nam. These mountainous regions offer spectacular landscapes, rare animal species, and are often covered by dense rainforests that are considered important ecosystems.

Cambodia is located in the tropics and has a hot and humid climate determined by the monsoon winds. The seasons can be roughly divided into a rainy and a dry season. The rainy season lasts from May to October and brings heavy rainfall, while the dry season runs from November to April and is characterized by cooler temperatures and less rain.

Cambodia's natural diversity is rich in flora and fauna. The tropical rainforests are home to a variety of plant species, including teak, bamboo and numerous orchids. The wildlife includes endangered species such as the

Indochinese tiger, the Asian elephant, gibbons, and various species of reptiles and birds. Protecting these natural resources is critical to preserving the country's biodiversity.

Overall, Cambodia presents itself as a country of great geographical diversity and natural beauty, known not only for its historical treasures, but also for its rich environment and scenic splendor that attracts visitors from all over the world.

History I: Ancient Civilizations and the Khmer Empire

The Khmer Empire, one of the most impressive and culturally significant empires in Southeast Asia, shaped the history of Cambodia for centuries. Its origins can be traced back to the 6th century, when the area around present-day Angkor in northwestern Cambodia began to develop. The name "Khmer" itself comes from the people who founded this empire and whose culture still shapes the national sense of identity today.

The heyday of the Khmer Empire stretched from the 9th to the 15th century and was marked by a remarkable cultural and architectural development. Under rulers such as King Suryavarman II, the empire experienced its greatest expansion, building monumental temples such as Angkor Wat, which remains the largest religious structure in the world today. These temple complexes, including Angkor Thom and Ta Prohm, bear witness to the amazing Khmer architecture and engineering skills and their deep connection to Hinduism and later Buddhism.

The Khmer Empire was known not only for its impressive buildings, but also for its progressive administration and cultural achievements. The Khmer developed a sophisticated irrigation system that made it possible to cultivate the central lowlands with their fertile soils and support a thriving agriculture. Trade and culture flourished, and Angkor became a major cultural and religious center, attracting pilgrims and scholars from all over Southeast Asia.

In the 13th century, the Khmer Empire experienced another heyday under Jayavarman VII, expanding its borders to Thailand, Laos and Viet Nam. The capital Angkor Thom was built, an impressive city center with monumental temples and royal palaces. Art and literature flourished, and the Khmer language in particular developed into a literary language for religious texts and poetry.

The decline of the Khmer Empire in the 15th century marked the beginning of a period of retreat and fragmentation. Internal conflicts, pressure from neighboring kingdoms and climatic changes that led to droughts visibly weakened the empire. The capital was abandoned, and Angkor was gradually reclaimed by nature until it was rediscovered by European explorers in the 19th century.

The history of the Khmer Empire and its ancient civilization remains a fascinating chapter in the history of Southeast Asia and is a significant legacy for modern Cambodia. The temples of Angkor and the cultural traditions of the Khmer are not only tourist attractions, but also symbols of the creative and spiritual height of the ancient kingdom, which has left behind a rich and complex history.

History II: Colonial Rule and Independence

In the 19th century, Cambodia experienced a phase of colonization by the French Empire, which had already gained a foothold in the neighboring countries of Southeast Asia. During the late 19th century, the French began to dominate the country politically, leaving the Khmer king as nominal ruler but taking effective control of the administration, economy, and legal system. This colonial rule brought significant changes to Cambodia, including the introduction of the French education system and administrative structures, which remained formative until the country's independence.

The colonial period was characterized by economic exploitation, especially in the area of agriculture and natural resources. French companies used plantation farming and monocultures to produce rice, rubber and other agricultural products, leading to social inequalities and dependencies. At the same time, colonial rule also brought some modernization and urbanization to Cambodia, with cities such as Phnom Penh becoming centers of trade and administration.

During World War II, Cambodia was briefly occupied by Japanese forces after France was defeated by Germany. The Japanese occupation left a mixed memory, as it temporarily weakened the influence of the French on the one hand, but also led to economic instability and political uncertainty on the other.

After the end of World War II and the withdrawal of the Japanese occupation, France re-established its control over Cambodia. However, in the late 1940s, a movement for independence began, led by nationalist forces such as Norodom Sihanouk, who played an important role in negotiating the country's independence. In 1953, Cambodia finally gained complete independence from France, having previously held the status of an autonomous state within the French Union.

The era of independence marked a new chapter in Cambodia's history, as the country began to develop its own political institutions and form a new national identity. Norodom Sihanouk, who served as both king and political leader, shaped this period and sought a policy of neutrality and internal peace. Despite these efforts, Cambodia remained politically unstable, leading to political upheaval and the rise of the Khmer Rouge regime in the decades that followed.

The period of colonial rule and subsequent independence was marked by profound changes and challenges that laid the foundation for Cambodia's modern history. The memory of this time is both culturally and politically significant and continues to have an impact on the societies of Southeast Asia today.

Story III: The Khmer Rouge era and its effects

The Khmer Rouge era in Cambodia, under the leadership of Pol Pot, marks one of the darkest and most tragic periods in the country's history. After defeating the pro-American regime in the civil war, the Khmer Rouge took control of Cambodia in 1975 and immediately began radical social, economic and political experiments. Their goal was to create an agrarian, communist society based on the idea of total equality and a retreat into rural communities.

In the first months of their rule, urban centers were evacuated and their inhabitants were forcibly taken to the countryside to work in collective labor camps. The Khmer Rouge pursued a policy of forced labor and tried to radically transform the entire Cambodian society. Educational institutions were closed, money was abolished and religion was banned. People were forced to engage in simple agricultural activities, while any form of intellectualism or urban lifestyle was brutally suppressed. The effects of this policy were devastating. It is estimated that between 1.7 and 2 million people died during the Khmer Rouge rule, which is about a quarter of the population at the time. The victims died of famine, disease, overwork and political persecution. Members of the intellectual class, members of minorities and people who were seen as political opponents were particularly targeted.

The Khmer Rouge also committed systematic human rights violations, including torture, mass executions and the establishment of prison camps such as Tuol Sleng (S-21) in Phnom Penh, where thousands of people were tortured and killed. These atrocities were later classified as genocide and crimes against humanity by an international tribunal.

The Khmer Rouge era ended in 1979 when Vietnamese troops occupied Cambodia and drove the Khmer Rouge out of urban areas. A civil war followed, which lasted until the 1990s and left deep social and political wounds. It was not until 1991 that a provisional political solution was found, which led to a new constitution and the establishment of a transitional government.

The effects of the Khmer Rouge era are still felt today. The country continues to struggle with the traumatic memories of this dark time as efforts to reconcile, justice, and build a democratic society move forward. The memorials and museums such as the Tuol Sleng Genocide Museum serve as a reminder of the victims and a reminder for future generations not to forget history and to work for peace and justice.

Politics and Government: Modern Cambodia

Modern Cambodia is a constitutional monarchy with a parliamentary form of government. Since the adoption of the new constitution in 1993, the country has had a political structure based on the principle of separation of powers. The King of Cambodia, currently Norodom Sihamoni, is the symbolic head of the state, while political power is exercised by a democratically elected government.

Cambodia's political system is shaped by the dominant role of the Cambodian People's Party (CPP), which has dominated the political landscape since the 1980s under the leadership of Hun Sen. Hun Sen, a former Khmer Rouge commander, is one of the world's longest-serving prime ministers and has played a central role in Cambodian politics since the 1980s.

The legislature is exercised through the bicameral system of parliament, which consists of the National Assembly (Lower House) and the Senate (Upper House). The National Assembly is elected every five years by universal suffrage, with the CPP traditionally holding an overwhelming majority of seats. The Senate consists of 62 members, of which two-thirds are appointed by the members of the National Assembly and one-third by the King.

Cambodia's political environment is characterised by challenges such as corruption, limited political freedoms and limited freedom of expression. The independence of the judiciary is often questioned, and political opposition parties and independent media are regularly under pressure. Human rights organizations regularly report cases of political repression and restrictions on freedom of assembly and expression.

International relations play an important role in Cambodia's foreign policy, with the country maintaining close ties with China, Viet Nam and other regional actors. Economic development and security cooperation are central issues in foreign policy, with Cambodia being a member of regional organizations such as ASEAN (Association of Southeast Asian Nations) and striving to play an active role in international forums.

In recent years, Cambodia has experienced rapid economic development, driven by investments in the tourism sector, textile industry, and other areas. This development has led to the growth of urban centres, while at the same time challenges such as poverty, unequal income distribution and environmental problems remain.

Cambodia's political future remains changing in the face of these challenges and dynamic regional and global forces. Efforts to promote political reforms, the protection of human rights and the promotion of transparent governance are crucial for the country's long-term stability and development.

Economy and Development: Opportunities and Challenges

Cambodia's economy has undergone a remarkable development in recent decades, which is characterized by various opportunities and challenges. After years of civil war and political instability, the country has experienced a rapid economic recovery since the 1990s. Key sectors of the economy are tourism, the textile industry, agriculture and the construction industry.

The tourism sector has become one of Cambodia's most important economic sectors, boosted by the country's rich cultural heritage, especially the temples of Angkor. Millions of visitors flock to Cambodia annually, which has led to a significant increase in foreign exchange earnings and job creation in the service sector.

The textile industry is another important sector of the Cambodian economy, which mainly benefits from foreign investment and proximity to global markets. Numerous foreign companies have set up production facilities in Cambodia to take advantage of the cheap labor costs and trade preferences that the country enjoys.

Despite increasing industrialization and urbanization, agriculture remains a central economic sector. Rice cultivation is of particular importance and Cambodia is one of the largest rice producers in the region. Smallholder farmers continue to dominate the agricultural sector, but it is challenged by seasonal droughts, land grabbing, and limited access to modern agricultural technologies and finance.

The construction industry is booming in the country's urban centers, especially in Phnom Penh and Sihanoukville, where there is a growing demand for apartments, office buildings, and infrastructure projects. Chinese investment has made a significant contribution to the development of construction, with large construction projects and real estate developments shaping the cityscape.

Despite these economic successes, Cambodia faces considerable challenges. A high dependence on foreign investment and tourism, together with a low diversification of the economy, makes the country vulnerable to external shocks such as global economic crises or political unrest. Corruption and a lack of the rule of law also remain significant barriers to sustainable growth and development of the private sector.

The government has taken steps to push ahead with economic reforms and create a favorable investment climate. This includes efforts to improve infrastructure, promote the private sector and strengthen institutional capacity. International development partners such as the World Bank and the International Monetary Fund are supporting Cambodia in these efforts with financial support and technical assistance.

The future of Cambodia's economy depends on the country's ability to address the challenges while taking advantage of the opportunities offered by a young population and strategic geographical location. Promoting sustainable development, creating jobs and strengthening social security will be crucial to secure the country's long-term prosperity potential.

Society and Culture: Traditions and Social Structures

Cambodia's society and culture are deeply rooted in a rich history and diverse traditions that have evolved over centuries. The Khmer culture, shaped by Hindu and Buddhist influences, forms the foundation of the national identity. Family and community play a central role in the social fabric, with traditional values such as respect for the elderly and social harmony being strong.

Cambodia is a multicultural society with a variety of ethnic groups, including Khmer, Cham, Chinese, and ethnic minorities such as the Khmer Loeu. This diversity is reflected in the language, religion, and cultural practices that contribute to the country's cultural landscape. The Khmer language is the official language and is spoken by the majority of the population, while minority languages such as Cham and various dialects are common in rural areas.

Religion plays an important role in the daily life of the people in Cambodia. Theravada Buddhism is the dominant religion, practiced by about 95% of the population. Monasteries and pagodas are important spiritual centers and serve both religious and social purposes.

In addition to Buddhism, there is a small Muslim minority, which is mainly found among the Cham, as well as Christian communities that make up a small part of the population.

Traditional arts and crafts play a significant role in Cambodian culture. Khmer art is known for its sculptures, murals, and textiles, which often depict religious or mythological themes. Traditional dances such as the classical Khmer Apsara dance drama are an important cultural heritage that expresses the mythological stories and historical events of the country.

Social life is characterized by rituals and celebrations, which are often associated with religious festivals and seasons. The Khmer New Year (Chaul Chnam Thmey) and the Water Festival (Bon Om Touk) are two of the most significant celebrations that celebrate community and traditions. Family plays a central role in Cambodian life, with strong intergenerational bonds and an emphasis on mutual support and care.

Modern developments and global influences have shaped Cambodia's cultural landscape, with young people increasingly adopting Western pop culture, technology, and educational opportunities. Cities like Phnom Penh are centers of social change, where modern lifestyles meet traditional values and a vibrant cultural scene emerges.

Despite these changes, traditional values and cultural practices remain deeply rooted in Cambodian society, which embodies a unique blend of continuity and adaptability. The preservation and promotion of this cultural diversity and traditions is crucial for strengthening national identity and the cohesion of a society that continues to face new social and global challenges.

Religions: Buddhism and other faiths

The religions in Cambodia reflect a diverse and rich spiritual landscape that is strongly influenced by the country's history and culture. The dominant faith is Theravada Buddhism, which is practiced by about 95% of the population. This form of Buddhism, which is based on the teachings of the historical Buddha Siddhartha Gautama, was introduced by monks from Sri Lanka in the 13th century and has had a profound influence on the cultural, social and spiritual life of Cambodia ever since.

Monasteries and pagodas are central institutions of Buddhism that fulfill not only religious, but also social and educational functions. Buddhist monks play a significant role in the community by providing spiritual guidance as well as providing social services such as education and charity. The monastic order is hierarchically organized, with novices and fully ordained monks taking a vow of devotion to Buddhist principles.

In addition to Buddhism, there is a Muslim minority in Cambodia, mainly among the Cham. Islam was introduced to the country in the 12th century and has established a distinct community with its own mosques, religious schools, and social customs. The Cham practice a Sunni Islam and follow the teachings of the Koran as well as local traditions.

Christianity is another religious minority in Cambodia that was introduced mainly by missionaries and has a small but growing following. The Catholic Church is the most prominently represented, although there are also Protestant communities. Christian institutions are active in education and social support and contribute to the diversity of the religious landscape.

Traditional religions and animistic belief systems are still present in rural areas, where local spirits and deities are worshipped to ensure protection and prosperity. These forms of faith are often associated with agricultural practices and seasons that reflect the spiritual and cultural heritage of the Khmer people.

Religious tolerance and the coexistence of different faiths are a characteristic feature of Cambodian society, which has been shaped by centuries of interaction and cultural exchange. Despite political and societal changes, religion remains an integral part of Cambodia's daily life and national identity, with monasteries, pagodas, and religious celebrations continuing to play a central role in the social fabric.

Education system and social services

The education system and social services in Cambodia face multiple challenges and have developed continuously since the early years of the country's independence. The education system is structured by a three-tier model, consisting of primary, secondary and higher education. Primary education is free and compulsory for children aged 6 to 12, but there are still high enrolment rates and significant regional differences in access and quality of education.

Secondary education is divided into two cycles: a three-year cycle and a two-year cycle. Access to secondary education is also limited, especially in rural areas and among disadvantaged groups. The quality of educational institutions varies widely, with urban schools often being better equipped and having more qualified teachers than schools in remote areas.

Higher education in Cambodia includes universities, colleges, and vocational schools. Universities are highly centralized and are mainly concentrated in Phnom Penh and other larger cities. Access to higher education is severely limited due to limited capacity and resources, resulting in high demand and fierce competition for study places.

The quality of higher education is also a challenge, with curricula often outdated and the lack of qualified lecturers being another obstacle. Despite these challenges, efforts are underway to modernize the education system, including introducing new curricula, training teachers, and improving infrastructure.

Social services in Cambodia include health care, social security, and support programs for populations in need. The country's health system has improved since the 1990s, with life expectancy increasing and child mortality rates falling. Nevertheless, challenges remain, such as limited access to health services in rural areas and deficiencies in health infrastructure.

Social safety nets are limited and include government programs such as the provision of food assistance and financial assistance to families in need. Non-governmental organizations (NGOs) play an important role in providing social services and supporting community development projects, especially in rural and remote areas.

Cambodia faces the challenge of further improving education and social services in order to promote the quality of life and equal opportunities for all citizens. Investments in educational infrastructure, teacher training and strengthening social safety nets are essential to drive the country's sustainable development and promote social inclusion.

Art and Literature: Insights into Cambodian Creativity

The art and literature in Cambodia is a rich heritage that offers deep insights into the cultural creativity and historical development of the country. Khmer art has a long tradition, dating back to the Angkor Empire, where impressive temples and sculptures were created that depict both religious and mythological themes. An outstanding example is the temple complex of Angkor Wat, which is considered not only an architectural masterpiece, but also a symbol of Khmer civilization.

Traditional Khmer art includes sculptures, murals, ceramics, and textiles, often inspired by religious motifs and nature. The Apsara dances are a well-known example of the connection between art and religion, expressing mythological stories through elegant movements and costumes. These artistic expressions have undergone continuous development over the centuries and are still present in the modern Cambodian art scene today.

Literature in Cambodia also has a long history, with classic works such as the Reamker, a Cambodian version of the Indian epic Ramayana, occupying a significant place. These literary works were often handed down orally and later recorded in palm leaf manuscripts. The Khmer script, a form of the Indian Devanagari script, has historically been used to record religious texts, stories, and historical chronicles.

In modern times, Cambodian literature has experienced a renaissance, with writers and poets exploring new themes and styles. The literature often reflects the social and political changes in the country, including the impact of the civil war and the Khmer Rouge era on society. Writers such as U Sam Ouer and Kong Bunchhoeun have created important works that preserve cultural heritage and address contemporary issues.

The modern art scene in Cambodia is dynamic and diverse, with artists working in the fields of painting, sculpture, photography, and performance art. Urban hubs like Phnom Penh are hubs of artistic innovation, where galleries, art exhibitions, and cultural events foster the creative community. Cambodian artists often draw on traditional motifs and themes while exploring new techniques and expressions that reflect global influences.

The promotion of art and literature is an integral part of Cambodia's cultural identity and national heritage, supported by efforts by government agencies, NGOs and cultural institutions. The preservation and promotion of these creative expressions is crucial for strengthening national identity and cultural exchange, both within the country and internationally.

Architecture: Temples and historical buildings

Cambodia's architecture is known worldwide for its imposing temples and historic structures that reflect a rich cultural tradition and spiritual depth. The highlight of these architectural masterpieces is undoubtedly in the temple ruins of Angkor, especially the majestic Angkor Wat. This huge temple complex, built in the 12th century under King Suryavarman II, is the largest religious structure in the world and a UNESCO World Heritage Site. With its unique construction that includes a complex array of galleries, towers and religious symbols, Angkor Wat embodies the height of Khmer architecture and symbolizes the cosmological ideas of Hinduism.

In addition to Angkor Wat, other significant temples can be found in the Angkor complex, including Bayon Temple with its iconic towers decorated with giant stone faces. The Ta Prohm Temple, known for its ruins overgrown with roots, shows the harmonious integration of architecture and nature. These temples testify to the amazing craftsmanship and artistic talent of the Khmer builders, who erected complex structures made of stone that are still admired today.

Outside of Angkor, there are other historical buildings in Cambodia that reflect the cultural and architectural diversity of the country. In Phnom Penh, the capital, stands the Royal Palace, a magnificent example of traditional Khmer architecture with its gilded roofs and intricately carved decorations. Next to the Royal Palace is the Silver Pagoda, whose floor is covered with 5,000 silver tiles and houses many significant Buddhist statues.

Other regions of the country are home to smaller temples and sacred sites, often cared for and revered by local communities. These buildings, often constructed of wood and bamboo, show the diversity of regional architectural styles and the adaptability of Khmer architecture to local environments and climatic conditions.

Modern architecture in Cambodia shows a mix of traditional elements and contemporary design, especially in urban centers, where skyscrapers and modern buildings dominate the cityscape. Despite this development, the preservation and restoration of the historic temples and buildings remains a central concern in order to preserve the country's cultural heritage and preserve it for future generations.

Language: Khmer and regional dialects

The Khmer language is the official language of Cambodia and is spoken by the vast majority of the population, approximately 97%. It belongs to the Mon-Khmer language family and is mainly used in Cambodia, but also in some adjacent regions of Thailand and Vietnam. The Khmer alphabet consists of 33 consonants, 23 vowels and 12 independent vowels, with each character having a specific pronunciation and meaning.

In addition to Khmer, several regional dialects are spoken in Cambodia, which vary depending on geographical location and ethnicity. Some of the most significant dialects are the Phnom Penh dialect, which is spoken in the capital and surrounding areas, as well as the dialect of the coastal regions and the northern provinces. These dialects can have differences in pronunciation, vocabulary, and grammatical structure that are shaped by local traditions and historical influences.

The Khmer language has absorbed various influences throughout history, especially from Sanskrit and Pali, which were introduced by Buddhism. Many religious and

39

literary texts are written in Sanskrit or Pali, which has led to the development of specialized terminology in these areas. Despite these influences, Khmer has retained its own identity and established itself as an important means of cultural and national communication.

The promotion of the Khmer language is a central concern of the Cambodian government, which implements measures to strengthen and maintain the language, especially in the education and media sectors. Nevertheless, many ethnic minority groups face challenges in accessing education in their mother tongue, which can lead to a certain degree of linguistic diversity and language loss.

In recent decades, globalization and the increasing presence of digital media has led to an increased use of English and other world languages, especially among the younger generation and in urban areas. This has led to discussions about the preservation of the Khmer language and the need to protect it as an integral part of national identity and cultural diversity.

Traditional clothing and fashion

Traditional clothing and fashion in Cambodia reflect a rich cultural tradition that is deeply rooted in the country's history. A central element of traditional Khmer clothing is the sampot, a long wrap dress worn by both men and women. The Sampot is made from a single piece of fabric that is wrapped around the waist and shaped into a skirt, with the ends artfully draped over the shoulders. This traditional clothing is widely used both in everyday life and on special occasions such as festivals and ceremonies.

Women often wear a blouse called a sabai and decorative scarves, while men can pair the sampot with a shirt. The colors and patterns of the Sampot vary depending on the occasion and region, with certain designs having historical and spiritual meanings. Handmade embroidery and ornate embellishments are distinctive features of traditional clothing, demonstrating the artistic talent and craftsmanship of Khmer culture.

In addition to the Sampot, Cambodia's various ethnic communities are home to diverse traditional clothing styles that reflect local craftsmanship and cultural practices. These ethnic groups, such as the Cham and the

Khmer Loeu, often wear specific robes and jewelry that emphasize their ethnic identity and preserve generations of cultural heritage.

In modern times, the Cambodian fashion industry has evolved, with designers and fashion design schools combining traditional elements with contemporary design. Cities like Phnom Penh are hubs of creative fashion, where local designers showcase their collections and integrate international influences. Cambodian silk, known as "hol", is a sought-after material for traditional and modern clothing, prized for its softness, shine and artistic workmanship.

The promotion of traditional clothing and fashion is an important aspect of Cambodia's cultural identity, promoted by government initiatives to support craftsmanship and traditional manufacturing techniques. The preservation and transmission of these cultural practices is crucial to the preservation of Cambodian culture and the promotion of a unique cultural heritage that is valued both nationally and internationally.

Cuisine: The diversity of Cambodian gastronomy

Cambodian cuisine offers a fascinating variety of aromas and flavors that are heavily influenced by local ingredients, cultural traditions, and historical influences. Rice is the staple food and is used in many dishes, often as an accompaniment to meat, fish or vegetables. One of the most famous Cambodian specialties is amok, a steamed curry dish often made with fish or chicken and seasoned with coconut milk, galangal, kaffir lime leaves, and spices like turmeric and chili.

Fish plays a central role in Cambodian cuisine, especially in rural areas along the rivers and lakes. A popular way to prepare it is the fish on a spit, which is grilled and served with a spicy sauce of lime, garlic, chili and sugar. In coastal areas, seafood such as crab, shrimp and squid are widely available and are often used in soups or fried dishes.

Cambodian salads, such as the green mango salad with fish sauce, lime and pepperoni, offer a refreshing balance of sweet, sour and spicy flavours. Local herbs and vegetables such as coriander, mint, basil, eggplant and beans are indispensable in many dishes, adding to the variety and complexity of flavours.

Street food is common in Cambodia and offers a variety of inexpensive and tasty options, including noodle soups like kuy teav and fried rice dishes like bai sach chrouk, which is served with grilled pork and pickled vegetables. Markets such as the Central Market in Phnom Penh are hotspots for culinary experiences, where visitors can sample local specialties, including fried insects such as grasshoppers and silkworms, which are a traditional source of protein.

Cambodian dessert includes sweet treats such as sticky rice with mango, which is made with coconut milk and sugar, as well as fruit sorbets and rice cakes. The use of fresh fruits such as mangoes, durian and dragon fruit is common in sweet cuisine and provides a refreshing addition to the spicy main courses.

Cambodian gastronomy is enriched by its diversity, which includes regional specialties and culinary traditions. Food preparation is often a collaborative activity that strengthens social bonds and promotes cultural identity. Despite increasing globalization and the influence of international cuisines, Cambodian cuisine remains a cornerstone of national identity and a source of proud cultural heritage.

Music and Dance: Traditional Forms and Modern Interpretations

Music and dance in Cambodia are central expressions of the country's cultural identity and history. Traditional Khmer musical instruments include the pin peat orchestra, which consists of drums, gong cymbals, xylophones, and other percussive instruments often played at royal ceremonies and religious festivals. This music is highly rhythmic and ritualized, and each melody and rhythm has a specific symbolic meaning.

Traditional dances, such as the Apsara dances, are an outstanding example of the combination of music and movement in Khmer culture. The Apsara dances are elegant and graceful, with dancers using elaborate hand gestures and postures to depict mythological stories and spiritual concepts. These dance forms have been cultivated for centuries and are considered a living heritage of Khmer art and culture.

Modern interpretations of traditional music and dance forms are widespread in Cambodia, especially in urban centers such as Phnom Penh. Young artists and choreographers combine traditional elements with contemporary styles and themes to create new forms of expression that reflect the diversity and dynamism of Khmer culture. This development has led to a renewal of interest in traditional music and dance and contributes to the promotion of cultural identity.

In addition to traditional forms, Cambodian musicians and dancers have also incorporated international influences into their work, resulting in a fusion of different styles and genres. Pop music and hip-hop are popular with the younger generation, while traditional instruments and melodies are often incorporated into contemporary compositions. This diversity reflects the cultural openness and creativity that is increasingly found in the Cambodian art scene.

The promotion of music and dance is supported by cultural institutions and government initiatives that promote programs to train young talent and preserve traditional arts. Festivals and cultural events provide platforms for artists to showcase their talent and celebrate the diversity of Cambodian culture. Music and dance therefore remain not only artistic forms of expression, but also living symbols of the identity and cohesion of the people of Cambodia.

Festivals and Celebrations: Seasons of Joy

Festivals and celebrations play a central role in Cambodia's social and cultural life, with traditional customs and religious rituals celebrated throughout the year. One of the most significant festivals is the Khmer New Year, known as "Chaul Chnam Thmey", which is celebrated over three days in April. During this time, people return to their home villages to visit their families and participate in religious ceremonies that symbolize purification and renewal.

Another important festival is the Water Festival or "Bon Om Touk", which marks the beginning of the dry season and the reverse flow of the Tonle Sap River. These celebrations include boat regattas on the river and a lively atmosphere full of music, dancing and local specialties along the waterfronts. Attracting thousands of visitors from home and abroad every year, Bon Om Touk is a highlight in Cambodia's calendar of festivities.

Religious holidays also play an important role, including the Vesakh festival, which celebrates the birthday, enlightenment, and death of the Buddha. On this day, believers visit the temples to make offerings and participate in meditative practices. The Kathina ceremony at the end of

Buddhist Lent is also an important event where communities come together to honor monks and promote the tradition of generosity.

Cambodia's ethnic minorities celebrate their own traditional festivals, often associated with agricultural seasons and cultural lore. For example, the Cham community celebrates "Chol Chnam", which is similar to their New Year, while the Khmer Loeu have various rituals that reflect their spiritual connection to nature and their ancestors.

Modern celebrations, such as music festivals and cultural events, have gained prominence in recent years, with international and local artists sharing the stages and showcasing the diversity of Cambodia's art scene. These events promote cultural exchange and raise awareness of the rich diversity of traditions and customs in the country.

Cambodia's holidays and festivities are not only opportunities for joy and community, but also opportunities to experience and celebrate the deep connection of the people to their history, their culture and their spiritual dimension. They are an expression of a living cultural identity that is cultivated and passed on through generations.

Crafts and craftsmanship: preservation of cultural heritage

Crafts and craftsmanship play a crucial role in Cambodia in preserving cultural heritage and promoting local identities. Traditional craftsmanship spans a variety of disciplines, including textiles, ceramics, wood carving, silversmithing, and more. Each of these art forms has its own long history and is closely linked to Cambodian culture and religious practices.

In the rural areas of the country, traditional crafts are often passed down by hand from generation to generation. Textiles, such as the famous "Krama" cotton scarves, are made on traditional looms and are not only practical, but also a symbol of Cambodian identity. These scarves are often made in vibrant colors and patterns that reflect local motifs and geometric designs.

Ceramic art in Cambodia has a long tradition that dates back to the times of the Khmer Empire. Products such as clay vessels and sculptures are shaped by hand and decorated with traditional motifs, often depicting religious and mythological stories. In the workshops in villages such as Kampong Chhnang and Siem Reap, visitors can admire and learn the craftsmanship of local artists.

Wood carving is another significant art form that is often used to decorate temples and pagodas. Complex carvings of deities, animals, and mythological scenes adorn the structures, serving as an expression of the spiritual depth and craftsmanship of Khmer artists. These works of art are not only aesthetically pleasing, but also a testament to the ongoing tradition of craftsmanship in Cambodia.

Silversmithing is also a cherished tradition, with fine silver jewellery often made for religious ceremonies and special occasions. The art of silversmithing requires precise skills and is cultivated by specialized craftsmen over generations. Silver amulets and jewelry with traditional symbols are popular souvenirs for visitors and an expression of Cambodian artistry.

The Cambodian government and non-governmental organizations are actively working to protect and promote traditional handicrafts by creating training opportunities for young artists and promoting markets for the sale of handmade products. These initiatives help to preserve the country's cultural heritage and ensure the survival of traditional craftsmanship, which plays an essential role in the social and economic fabric of Cambodian communities.

Folklore and legends: stories from times gone by

Folklore and legends play a significant role in Cambodia's rich cultural landscape, offering insights into the country's deep-rooted beliefs and traditions. Many of the stories and myths are closely linked to Khmer mythology, which includes a variety of deities, heroes, and mystical creatures. One of the most famous figures is the mythical monkey king Hanuman, who plays a central role in many traditional tales and is revered for his bravery and wisdom.

Another significant figure in Khmer folklore is Neak Ta, the spirit of the earth and nature, who is revered in rural communities to provide protection and fertility. Legends of Neak Ta are often associated with local customs such as harvesting and spiritual practices that reflect people's deep belief in natural order and balance.

The stories of Preah Thong and Neang Neak are also widely shared, telling the adventures of two lovers who go through trials and obstacles to preserve their love. These epic tales are a reflection of the Khmer idea of heroic bravery and unwavering loyalty, often performed in theatrical performances and songs.

Cambodian folklore also includes stories of spirits and supernatural beings such as Apsara, beautiful celestial dancers depicted in the temple walls of Angkor Wat, believed to be messengers of the gods. These mystical figures inspire art, dance and music and are an integral part of Cambodia's cultural identity.

In addition to the mythological tales, there are also historical legends that surround events and personalities from the rich history of the Khmer Empire. Stories of kings, heroes and conquerors offer insights into the political and social developments that have shaped Cambodia's history.

The preservation and transmission of folklore and legends is often done orally through generations and is an essential part of the cultural education and identity of the Khmer. Through stories, songs and rituals, these stories are kept alive and contribute to the connection of the communities with their past and their spiritual world. Folklore is thus not just a collection of stories, but a window into the soul and faith of a people that preserves its history and identity through rich oral traditions.

Environment and Nature Conservation: The Challenge of Sustainability

Environmental protection and sustainability are an increasing challenge for Cambodia as the country faces a growing population, urbanization and pressure on natural resources. The diversity of ecosystems, from tropical rainforests to coastal ecosystems, makes Cambodia an ecologically rich country, but one that suffers from various environmental problems.

One of the biggest problems is deforestation, which is driven by both legal and illegal practices. This threatens not only biodiversity, but also the livelihoods of local communities that depend on forests. Government programs and international cooperation have helped curb deforestation, but challenges remain.

Protecting water resources is also crucial, especially in the face of climate change and increasing water pollution. One of the largest freshwater lakes in Southeast Asia, the Tonle Sap is an important ecosystem for fish and other aquatic life, but also for millions of people who depend on its fisheries. The sustainable management of these resources is crucial for Cambodia's future.

Nature conservation and the promotion of national parks and protected areas play an important role in the preservation of the country's biodiversity. Bokor National Park and Virachey Nature Reserve are examples of areas that are of great importance for both biodiversity and tourism. The management of these protected areas requires a balanced strategy that reconciles the needs of the environment with the economic and social interests of the communities.

The ecological footprint of tourism is also a challenge, as Cambodia is a popular tourist destination, especially because of its historical sites such as Angkor Wat. The sustainable tourism approach aims to minimize the negative impact on the environment and empower local communities by providing them with opportunities for income and education.

Cambodia faces the challenge of balancing economic growth and social development with the protection of its natural resources and the preservation of its unique environment. However, through international cooperation, government policy and the commitment of civil society, progress has been made in the field of environmental protection and sustainability, which gives hope for the future of the country.

Wildlife: Biodiversity in Cambodia

Cambodia's wildlife is characterized by an impressive diversity, ranging from the lush rainforests in the northeast to the coasts and rivers in the south. The country is home to numerous endangered species as well as unique ecosystems that need to be protected to ensure their long-term viability.

The tropical rainforests are home to some of the rarest and most endangered animal species in the world, including the Indochinese tiger and the Sunda clouded leopard. These majestic predators are symbols of the region's biodiversity, but they are also under great pressure from poaching and the loss of their natural habitat.

The Asian elephant is another characteristic animal of Cambodia, found both in the wild and in protected reserves such as Mondulkiri Province in the east of the country. These gentle giants play an important role in the ecosystem by contributing to the dispersal of seeds and shaping the forest through their behavior.

The diversity of birdlife in Cambodia is also remarkable, with over 600 registered species, including the Sarus Crane, one of the largest flying bird species in the world. The wetlands of Tonle Sap Lake and the Mekong River are important breeding grounds for migratory birds and waterfowl that arrive from more distant regions during the dry season.

Cambodia's waters are rich in life forms, including over 850 species of fish found in the country's rivers, lakes, and coastal waters. The Mekong River, one of the longest rivers in the world, is known for its fish diversity and supports the livelihoods of millions of people who depend on fishing.

However, the threat to Cambodia's wildlife comes not only from direct hunting and habitat loss, but also from the illegal wildlife trade industry, which poses a serious threat to many species. Tigers, elephants, and turtles are particularly endangered and are often hunted for their body parts and the exotic pet market.

Conservation in Cambodia is driven by government programs, international cooperation, and the commitment of environmental organizations that work to preserve endangered species and their habitats. By protecting protected areas and promoting sustainable practices, there is hope that Cambodia's unique wildlife will be preserved for future generations.

National parks and protected areas

National parks and protected areas play a crucial role in the conservation of natural diversity and environmental quality in Cambodia. The country has several important protected areas that are recognized both nationally and internationally. One of the most famous is the Virachey National Park in the northeast of the country, which covers an area of over 3,300 square kilometers and serves as a refuge for endangered species such as the Indochinese tiger and the Asian elephant. The park is also home to a rich variety of birds and is of cultural significance to the indigenous communities of the region.

Another important protected area is the Bokor National Park, which is located in the southern foothills of the Dâmrei Mountains. This area is known for its diverse flora and fauna, as well as historical sites built during the French colonial period. The park attracts tourists who want to explore the natural beauty and historical sights of the area.

Kirirom National Park in southwestern Cambodia offers a retreat for visitors who want to enjoy the park's mountain landscapes, waterfalls, and hiking trails. This park is a popular destination for local tourists as well as nature lovers who want to experience the country's rich biodiversity and landscape diversity.

The management and conservation of these protected areas is carried out by the Ministry of Environment and other competent authorities, which implement programmes to monitor wildlife populations and combat poaching. International organizations and non-governmental organizations also contribute to the protection of Cambodia's natural resources through financial support and technical assistance for conservation projects.

The challenges for the protected areas include sustainable financing, coping with the pressures of illegal logging and poaching, and promoting ecological education and awareness among the population. Despite these challenges, national parks and protected areas make a decisive contribution to the conservation of biodiversity and the promotion of sustainable tourism in Cambodia, making them of great importance both ecologically and economically.

Phnom Penh: The capital through the ages

Phnom Penh, the capital of Cambodia, is a fascinating testimony to the country's eventful history and dynamic development. Founded in 1434 by King Ponhea Yat, the city underwent numerous transformations under various rulers and colonial powers. During the Khmer rule, Phnom Penh was an important trading center that flourished culturally through the construction of temples and royal palaces.

With the influence of the French in the late 19th century, Phnom Penh experienced a modernization that is reflected in the architecture of the colonial era. Magnificent French-style buildings, including Notre-Dame Cathedral and the old post office, still characterize the cityscape today.

During the 20th century, Phnom Penh experienced an era of political change and challenges. Under the rule of the Khmer Rouge in the 1970s, the city suffered severe destruction and humanitarian crises that left deep scars on the city. The brutal effects of this period, including depopulation and loss of cultural heritage, have left a strong mark on the city and its inhabitants.

Since the 1990s, Phnom Penh has experienced a period of reconstruction and economic recovery. The city has become an important center for trade, education and tourism. Modern skyscrapers, shopping malls, and business districts reflect the rapid growth and urbanization that characterize the city.

Today, Phnom Penh is a vibrant metropolis with a rich cultural scene and a growing middle class. Historic sites like the Royal Palace and the National Museum attract visitors, while markets like the Central Market and Russian Market are the beating heart of urban life.

The challenges facing Phnom Penh continue to include urbanisation, infrastructure renewal and tackling social inequalities. The government and local initiatives are working to address these challenges, while Phnom Penh continues to play a key role in Cambodia's economic and cultural life and asserts itself as a dynamic capital city through the ages.

Siem Reap: Gateway to the Temples of Angkor

Siem Reap, a picturesque city in northwestern Cambodia, is known worldwide as the gateway to the fascinating temples of Angkor, a UNESCO World Heritage Site. Siem Reap's history goes back a long way, with historical roots dating back to the founding of the Khmer Empire in the 9th century. In the centuries that followed, the region experienced a period of prosperity under various Khmer rulers, which was characterized by the construction of magnificent temples and monumental structures.

However, it is only in the last few decades that the modern city of Siem Reap has become a major tourist center, attracting millions of visitors every year. The main attraction undoubtedly remains the Angkor Archaeological Park, which covers over 400 square kilometers and includes more than a thousand historic temples and religious monuments.

The most famous temple in the Angkor area is undoubtedly Angkor Wat, an architectural masterpiece and the largest religious monument in the world. With its impressive size and elaborate stonemasonry, Angkor Wat attracts visitors from all over the world who want to discover the rich history and spiritual significance of this impressive structure.

In addition to Angkor Wat, other temples such as Angkor Thom with the famous Bayon Temple, Ta Prohm with its tree-covered ruins and Banteay Srei with its finely crafted relief depictions are important sights in the Angkor complex.

Siem Reap has quickly become a hub for tourism, hospitality, and cultural activities. The city offers a wide range of accommodation, from luxury hotels to guesthouses, to suit the needs of all visitors. The Pub Street area is known for its lively nightlife, restaurants serving traditional Khmer cuisine, and souvenir shops.

Siem Reap's economic development is heavily based on the tourism sector, which creates jobs and contributes to the local economy. At the same time, mass tourism poses a challenge to the preservation of the sensitive temple complexes and the surrounding environment, which is why sustainable tourism practices are becoming increasingly important.

Siem Reap faces the challenge of finding the balance between preserving cultural heritage and promoting responsible tourism. Initiatives to preserve temples, educate local communities, and promote sustainable practices are critical to the city's future as a gateway to the temples of Angkor and a cultural gem of Cambodia.

Battambang and other major cities

Battambang, Cambodia's second-largest city, is known for its rich history, cultural diversity, and significant artistic traditions. It is located in the northwest of the country and is an important center for art, education and trade. The city was founded in the 11th century and has experienced an eventful history over the centuries, ranging from Khmer rule to the French colonial period.

Today, Battambang is a vibrant city known for its well-preserved French architecture and charming atmosphere. The tree-lined boulevards and colonial buildings dot the cityscape and attract both tourists and locals. Psar Nat Market is a vibrant hub of urban life, offering local produce, handicrafts and traditional Khmer cuisine.

In addition to Battambang, Cambodia has other significant cities, each with its own unique features and cultural treasures. Sihanoukville, located on the coast of the Gulf of Thailand, is an important center for international trade and tourism. The city is famous for its beautiful beaches and resorts that attract both local and foreign visitors.

The capital Phnom Penh is the political, economic and cultural center of the country. With a rich history dating back to ancient times, Phnom Penh offers a variety of attractions, including the Royal Palace, the National Museum, and the Tuol Sleng Genocide Museum, which commemorates the dark chapters of recent history.

Another important city is Kampong Cham, which is located on the banks of the Mekong River. This town is known for its traditional Khmer villages, fertile rice paddies, and laid-back way of life. Kampong Cham is also an important trading hub and a center for the production of agricultural products.

In recent years, these cities have evolved and become major players in Cambodia's economic development. The challenges they face include urbanization, infrastructure renewal, and addressing social inequalities. Nevertheless, they play a crucial role in Cambodia's cultural heritage and modern life, preserving indigenous traditions while contributing to the global diversity of cities.

Coastal towns: Beach paradises on the Gulf of Thailand

The coastal resorts along the Gulf of Thailand offer some of Cambodia's most beautiful beach paradises, attracting both locals and tourists alike. Sihanoukville, also known as Kampong Som, is one of the most famous coastal towns in the country. Originally founded as a small fishing village, Sihanoukville has developed into a major commercial and tourism center. The city is famous for its stunning beaches, including Ochheuteal Beach, Sokha Beach, and Independence Beach, which beckon with golden sands and clear waters.

Kep is another popular coastal spot known for its laid-back atmosphere and delicious seafood. Originally established as a retreat for French colonial officials, Kep is now known for its charming charm and historic colonial-era mansions. Kep National Park offers spectacular views of the sea and is a popular destination for hikers and nature lovers.

Kampot, although not located directly on the coast, is a picturesque town located on the banks of the Praek Tuek Chhu River, about 5 kilometers from the coast. Known for its French architecture and relaxed atmosphere,

Kampot is famous for its pepper, which is considered one of the best in the world. The city is a popular destination for travelers who want to experience the tranquility of the coastal region and the natural beauty of the river valley.

The development of coastal resorts has gained momentum in recent years, which has led to an increase in hotels, resorts and tourist facilities. The government and local communities are working to improve infrastructure while protecting the environment to preserve the natural beauty and attractiveness of the coastal region.

Tourists enjoy not only the gorgeous beaches and warm waters of the Gulf of Thailand, but also the variety of activities, ranging from water sports such as diving and snorkeling to boat trips to nearby islands. Cambodia's coastal resorts offer a unique blend of natural beauty, cultural heritage and modern comforts that make them a sought-after destination for visitors from all over the world.

Cambodian Islands: Idyllic Retreats

The Cambodian islands in the Gulf of Thailand offer idyllic retreats for travelers looking for unspoiled nature and a relaxing atmosphere. One of the most famous islands is Koh Rong, which is known for its white-sand beaches, crystal clear waters, and lush tropical vegetation. Koh Rong is the largest island in the country and has become a popular destination in recent years, especially for young backpackers and nature lovers.

Koh Rong Samloem, a smaller island south of Koh Rong, is famous for its quiet beaches and relaxed atmosphere. The island is less developed than Koh Rong and offers visitors an escape from the hustle and bustle of modern life. The secluded bays and pristine beaches make Koh Rong Samloem an ideal destination for romantic escapes and nature lovers looking to explore the beauty of the underwater world.

Other Cambodian islands such as Koh Thmei and Koh Ta Kiev also offer unique experiences in nature. Koh Thmei is part of the Ream National Park and is known for its diverse birdlife and pristine mangrove forests.

Visitors can explore nature trails, bird watch and relax in the tranquil atmosphere.

Koh Ta Kiev, on the other hand, is known for its rustic beach huts and simple way of life. The island is only accessible by boat and offers visitors a true Robinson Crusoe experience with simple accommodation, secluded beaches and unspoiled nature.

The development of the Cambodian islands has gained momentum in recent years, which has led to an increase in hotels, guesthouses and tourist facilities. Nevertheless, the government and local communities are working to protect the environment and promote sustainable tourism to preserve the natural beauty and appeal of the islands.

The Cambodian islands offer an escape from everyday life and the opportunity to experience the unspoiled beauty of tropical nature. With their rich marine diversity, picturesque sunsets and a relaxed atmosphere, the islands invite visitors to explore paradise and create unforgettable memories.

Temple of Angkor: A Wonder of the World in Detail

The temples of Angkor are undoubtedly one of the most impressive archaeological wonders in the world and an icon of Khmer culture and history. They cover an area of several square kilometers near the city of Siem Reap in Cambodia and include hundreds of temples, the most famous and emblematic of which is Angkor Wat.

Built in the 12th century under the reign of King Suryavarman II, Angkor Wat is the largest religious monument in the world and a masterpiece of Khmer architecture. The monumental structure is surrounded by a moat and rises majestically above the surrounding landscape. The structure consists of three concentric galleries and central towers that symbolize Mount Meru, the center of the universe in Hindu mythology.

In addition to Angkor Wat, there are a variety of other temples in the Angkor complex, each with its own unique architectural features and cultural significances. The Bayon Temple in the center of Angkor Thom is known for its massive stone face towers, believed to represent the face of King Jayavarman VII.

These iconic faces are a symbol of unity and compassion in Buddhist teachings.

Another notable temple is Ta Prohm, which is known for its union with nature, as it is entwined by mighty trees and roots. This interplay of stone and vegetation gives Ta Prohm a mystical and romantic atmosphere and has made it one of the most popular photo motifs in the Angkor complex.

The temples of Angkor are not only a historical heritage, but also an important religious center. They originally served as spiritual places for worship and meditation, both in Hinduism and Buddhism, depending on which religion was prevalent in Cambodia at the time.

The restoration and preservation of the temples of Angkor is an ongoing process supported by both Cambodian authorities and international organizations. Tourism plays a crucial role in funding these efforts, as it attracts visitors from all over the world to experience and admire Angkor's cultural heritage.

In recent years, the government of Cambodia has made increased efforts to improve the infrastructure around the Angkor facility and optimize the visitor experience. This includes expanding roads, upgrading visitor centers, and promoting sustainable tourism to preserve the unique beauty and historical significance of Angkor's temples for future generations.

Temple Walking Tour: Angkor Discovery Tour

The temple tour of Angkor offers a fascinating discovery tour of one of the most important historical sites in the world. The Angkor Archaeological Park covers about 400 square kilometers and is home to hundreds of temples, reservoirs, canals, and other archaeological structures dating back to the Khmer period, which flourished between the 9th and 15th centuries.

The walking tour often begins with the majestic Angkor Wat, the largest and most famous temple in the complex. Built in the 12th century by King Suryavarman II, Angkor Wat is an outstanding example of Khmer architecture and spiritual significance. The monumental structure, which symbolizes Mount Meru, is surrounded by a wide moat and consists of a series of galleries and towers intricately decorated with reliefs and sculptures.

From Angkor Wat, the tour often continues to Angkor Thom, the last capital of the Khmer Empire. Angkor Thom is known for its imposing south gate with the famous face towers that could represent the face of the king. Within the walls of Angkor Thom are other important temples such as the Bayon, known for its numerous huge face towers that look in all directions.

Another highlight of the temple walking tour is Ta Prohm, famous for its romantic and mystical atmosphere created by the overgrowth of trees and roots that embrace the ruins. This interplay of nature and architecture makes Ta Prohm one of the most popular photo motifs in Angkor.

In addition to these main temples, there are many other lesser-known temples and archaeological sites in the Angkor complex that are worth visiting. Temples such as Banteay Srei, known for its finely crafted relief depictions made of pink sandstone, or Preah Khan, a complex of temples, monasteries and royal residences, offer insights into the diversity and complexity of Khmer culture and architecture.

The temple walking tour requires time and planning to fully experience the beauty and historical significance of the Angkor site. The Government of Cambodia and international organizations are working together to preserve and restore this significant historical site to preserve it for future generations while promoting sustainable tourism.

Visiting the temples of Angkor is not only a trip down memory lane, but also an opportunity to experience the deep spiritual and cultural significance of this monumental site, which is a significant part of Cambodia's history and identity.

Places of worship off the beaten track

In addition to the famous temples of Angkor, Cambodia is also home to a variety of lesser-known places of worship that are off the beaten track and yet allow you to delve deep into the country's history and culture. These lesser-visited places offer visitors a unique opportunity to discover the diversity and richness of the Khmer civilization, away from the crowds and tourist hustle and bustle.

One of these hidden gems is the temple complex of Banteay Chhmar in northwestern Cambodia. This sprawling complex includes several temple ruins and is known for its imposing towers and rich reliefs depicting scenes from everyday life, mythological stories, and historical events. Banteay Chhmar was once a thriving city and an important center of the Khmer Empire, whose splendor can still be seen today in the ornate stonework and architecture.

Further south is Preah Vihear Temple, perched on a steep mountaintop and offering spectacular views over the surrounding countryside. This temple is particularly known for its location and well-preserved architecture and was an important religious and political center during the Angkor period. Preah Vihear is a UNESCO World Heritage Site and attracts visitors who appreciate the challenge of the steep climbs and the reward of the breathtaking views.

Not far from Siem Reap is the Temple of Beng Mealea, often referred to as the "lost temple" and a landscape of ruins jutting out of the jungle. Beng Mealea offers a unique experience for adventure seekers and history buffs who want to explore the remains of a once magnificent site overgrown with roots and vegetation.

Other lesser-known places of worship include temples such as Koh Ker, the former capital of the Khmer Empire, which is now surrounded by dense forests and exudes a mystical atmosphere. Koh Ker was briefly the capital under King Jayavarman IV and is home to temples with unique architectural features, including the seven-tiered pyramid temple of Prasat Thom.

Discovering these off-the-beaten-path places of worship often requires a little more time and planning, as they are not as easily accessible as Angkor's main attractions. Nevertheless, they offer unique insights into the history and culture of Cambodia, far away from mass tourism, and are a valuable contribution to understanding and appreciating the rich heritage of this fascinating country.

Royal Palaces and Residences

Cambodia's royal palaces and residences reflect the country's magnificent history and royal tradition, which dates back to the times of Khmer kings. Today, the Royal Palace in Phnom Penh is the center of royal activity and one of the country's most significant historical attractions. Built in the 19th century during the reign of King Norodom, it combines traditional Khmer architecture with French influences from the colonial era.

The royal palace covers an area of several hectares and includes several impressive buildings, including the throne room, which is used for official ceremonies and receptions. One of the country's most important places of worship, the Silver Pagoda is located within the palace complex and is known for its floor, which is covered with over 5,000 silver tiles, as well as the Emerald Buddha, a life-size statue made of baccarat crystal, which is venerated here.

In addition to the royal palace in Phnom Penh, there are other royal residences and palaces in other parts of the country that have historical and cultural significance. Siem Reap Palace, also known as the Royal Palace of Angkor, was once a royal residence during the reign of the Khmer kings and is close to the famous temples of Angkor.

The Royal Palace of Oudong, about 40 kilometers from Phnom Penh, was formerly the capital of the Khmer Empire and still houses remnants of royal structures and stupas that attract visitors to explore the history and spiritual significance of the place.

The royal palaces and residences of Cambodia are not only historical sites, but also cultural centers that preserve the royal tradition and ceremonies associated with the monarchy. They are symbols of national identity and play an important role in official occasions and religious celebrations in the country. The preservation and care of these historic sites is a priority of the Cambodian government and international organizations to ensure their importance for future generations.

UNESCO World Heritage Sites in Cambodia

Cambodia is proud of its rich cultural heritage, which is internationally recognized by several UNESCO World Heritage Sites. These sites are testimony to the deep-rooted history and unique architectural achievements of the Khmer civilization that shaped the country between the 9th and 15th centuries.

The most famous and outstanding place is undoubtedly the temple complex of Angkor, which was declared a UNESCO World Heritage Site in 1992. Angkor Wat, the most famous structure within the complex, is a masterpiece of Khmer architecture and is considered the largest sacred structure in the world. In addition to Angkor Wat, the Angkor Archaeological Park includes numerous other temples and religious monuments, including the Bayon with its iconic face towers and Ta Prohm, the tree-covered "jungle temple".

Also on the UNESCO list is the Temple of Preah Vihear, perched on a hilltop in the province of Preah Vihear and offering spectacular panoramic views of the surrounding countryside. This temple is known for its unique location and well-preserved architecture, which symbolizes a connection between man and the divine.

Another UNESCO World Heritage Site is the Kingdom of Funan, which is considered Cambodia's earliest known civilization and controlled historic trade routes between India and China. The remains of these ancient sites, especially in the region of Angkor Borei, provide insight into the early cultural and political developments of the region.

In addition to these main sites, the list of UNESCO World Heritage Sites in Cambodia also includes the cultural landscape ensemble of Sambor Prei Kuk. Located in Kampong Thom Province, this archaeological site consists of over 100 temples built during the Chenla era between the 6th and 9th centuries. Sambor Prei Kuk is known for its early examples of Khmer architecture and religious practices, which offer an important insight into the cultural development of the region.

The recognition of these sites as UNESCO World Heritage Sites underlines their universal significance and value to humanity. The Cambodian government and international organizations are working together to preserve and restore these historical treasures to preserve them for future generations while promoting sustainable tourism.

Trade routes and historical sites

Cambodia's trade routes and historical sites bear witness to the country's rich history as a hub for trade and cultural exchange in Southeast Asia. Even in ancient times, Cambodia played an important role along the trade routes between India and China, with different cultures and civilizations passing through the country and leaving their mark.

An important trade route was the so-called Silk Road of the Sea, which connected maritime trade routes and enabled the exchange of goods, ideas and religious beliefs. Cambodia benefited from its strategic location on the Gulf of Thailand, which made it an important commercial center and encouraged the development of its cities and cultural centers.

The ancient city of Angkor Borei in southern Cambodia was a major trading center during the Funan period (1st to 6th centuries AD), prospering through trade with India and China. The remains of this city bear witness to an advanced urban society, with advanced irrigation systems and architectural structures that reflect both local and imported cultural influences.

During the Chenla and Khmer periods, trading activities continued and reached their peak under Khmer rule in the 9th to 15th centuries. The city of Koh Ker, briefly the capital of the Khmer Empire, was an important hub for the trade of precious raw materials such as precious stones and gold, which were transported from the surrounding areas to the royal palaces.

The temple town of Sambor Prei Kuk in Kampong Thom province is another testimony to the trading activities during the Chenla era (6th to 9th centuries). This archaeological site, consisting of over a hundred temples, was a cultural and religious center and served as an important link along the trade routes that promoted the exchange of goods and cultural ideas between India, China, and Southeast Asia.

The historical sites along Cambodia's trade routes offer insight into the region's complex history and the diversity of its cultural influences. They are not only witnesses of past trade relations, but also symbols of the country's cultural and economic heyday in different periods of its history.

Religious centers and pilgrimage sites

Religious centers and pilgrimage sites play a central role in Cambodia's cultural and spiritual landscape. The most impressive and well-known place is undoubtedly the temple complex of Angkor, especially Angkor Wat, which is considered the largest sacred structure in the world and is a significant center for the Buddhist faith. Built in the 12th century under the reign of King Suryavarman II, Angkor Wat combines architectural splendor with deeply religious symbolisms that reflect the cosmological worldview of the Khmer.

In addition to Angkor Wat, the Angkor Archaeological Park includes numerous other temples and religious sites, including Bayon Temple with its iconic face towers depicting Buddhas and Bodhisattvas. These temples served not only as places of prayer and meditation, but also as centers of royal worship and public life during Khmer rule.

Another significant religious site is the Temple of Preah Vihear, perched on a hilltop in the province of Preah Vihear and offering a unique panoramic view. This Hindu temple was built between the 9th and 12th centuries and symbolizes the connection between heaven and earth, making it an important pilgrimage destination for believers.

The Buddhist pagodas and monasteries throughout Cambodia also play an essential role in the country's religious life. In Phnom Penh, the imposing Silver Pagoda is located in the royal palace complex, known for its silver Bodhisattva statues and attracts thousands of pilgrims annually. In other cities such as Siem Reap and Battambang, pagodas such as Wat Bo and Wat Ek Phnom serve as important religious and cultural centers for the local community.

Cambodia's religious centres and pilgrimage sites are not only places of spiritual worship, but also important cultural and historical heritage. They reflect the deep attachment of the Khmer people to their religious beliefs and are living witnesses to the country's continuous spiritual practice and cultural development over centuries.

Khmer architecture: stylistic features and development

Khmer architecture is known for its impressive and monumental structures, which are a unique combination of religious symbolism, cosmological significance and technical sophistication. A prominent feature of Khmer architecture is the use of sandstone as the main building material, which allowed the architects to create complex relief representations and ornate carvings depicting the mythological and religious stories of the Khmer.

The peak of Khmer architecture is undoubtedly in the Angkor Empire (9th to 15th centuries), where monumental temples such as Angkor Wat, Bayon and Ta Prohm were built. Built under King Suryavarman II in the early 12th century, Angkor Wat embodies the classical Khmer architectural style with its central Temple Mount structure (Mandapa) and wraparound galleries adorned with bas-reliefs and devatas (divine beings).

A characteristic feature of Khmer architecture is the face towers, which are best preserved in the Bayon Temple. These towers are decorated with huge, smiling faces, which are interpreted as Lokesvara, a Buddhist divinity. The arrangement of the towers symbolizes the concept of Mount Meru, the cosmological center of the universe in Hindu and Buddhist mythology.

The architecture of the Khmer temples also shows a remarkable progressiveness in water management, with extensive systems of reservoirs and canals used not only for water supply but also for ritual and agricultural purposes. Examples include the Baray of Angkor Thom and the Srah Srang, a royal bathing spot.

Throughout Khmer history, architecture evolved, with elements from the Hindu pantheon being replaced by the influence of Theravada Buddhism. Temples such as Preah Khan and Pre Rup show this transitional phase, while later stylistic elements such as the Banteay-Srei temples set new artistic highlights with their fine relief work and smaller scales.

Khmer architecture is not only a reflection of the religious and cultural values of the Khmer civilization, but also an outstanding example of the technological and artistic achievements of this ancient society. It has had a profound impact on the architecture and art of Southeast Asia to this day and remains a fascinating object of study for archaeologists, historians and art lovers worldwide.

Influences of neighboring countries on Cambodian culture

Cambodian culture has been heavily influenced by neighboring countries throughout history, resulting in a multi-layered and multifaceted cultural landscape. Particularly formative were the influences from India, which came to the region through trade and the exchange of ideas during the heyday of the Angkor Empire (9th to 15th centuries) via Hinduism and later Buddhism. These religious teachings and artistic traditions left a lasting mark on Cambodia's architecture, art, and philosophy.

From the south, the Khmer also brought influences from the old Khmer empire of Funan (1st to 6th centuries), which was closely linked to the trade and maritime culture of the Indo-Pacific. Trade routes and maritime networks encouraged the exchange of goods, technologies, and cultural practices that influenced the social structure and Khmer way of life.

Both cultural and artisanal influences came from China, which were reinforced over the centuries by diplomatic relations and trade. This manifested itself in the adoption of ceramic techniques, silk production, and artistic motifs that enriched Cambodian arts and crafts.

Thai culture, especially during the Ayutthaya and Sukhothai eras, also had a strong influence on Cambodian culture, especially in architecture and certain religious practices. The political ties and cultural exchange processes between the two countries led to mutual influence in various areas of life.

French colonialism brought Western influences to Cambodia in the 19th century, which were reflected in architecture, education and social structure. This influence has also remained visible in modern Cambodian culture, especially in areas such as language, cuisine, and fashion.

Overall, Cambodian culture reflects a rich mix of indigenous traditions and the influences of its neighboring countries, which have formed a dynamic and fascinating cultural landscape throughout history. This cultural diversity and historical connections are essential elements of Cambodia's cultural heritage, which is of great importance both locally and internationally.

Modern art scene and contemporary artists

Cambodia's modern art scene is characterised by a growing diversity of contemporary artists who use both traditional and experimental methods to reflect on the country's social, political and cultural issues. After decades of oppression during the Khmer Rouge era and the post-conflict recovery, the Cambodian art scene has experienced a remarkable revival and development since the 1990s.

Modern art galleries and studios have gained prominence in cities such as Phnom Penh, Siem Reap and Battambang, with local and international artists alike helping to shape the artistic landscape. Some artists focus on traditional Cambodian techniques such as sculpture, painting, and ceramics, often combined with modern themes and styles, while others explore avant-garde approaches and new media.

The rise of art initiatives and institutions such as Sa Sa Art Projects, Romeet Gallery and Institut Français du Cambodge has helped to create a supportive environment for local artists and give them international visibility. These platforms not only promote artistic expression, but also serve as important cultural hubs for sharing and discussing contemporary art practices.

Some Cambodian artists have gained international recognition and regularly exhibit in galleries and museums around the world. Their works often address themes such as identity, memory, social justice, and cultural renewal, dealing with both personal experiences and collective traumas that have shaped the country.

Cambodia's contemporary art scene faces challenges such as limited resources, a lack of institutional support, and the need for sustainable market integration. Nevertheless, it remains dynamic and innovative, with artists who find a voice for the future of the country and its culture through their works.

Cambodian Literature: Past and Present

Cambodian literature has a rich history that dates back to ancient times and has evolved through different eras and influences. In the past, literature was strongly associated with religious texts, especially Buddhist scriptures, which played an important role in the cultural life of the country. These texts were often written on palm leaves and kept in the pagodas, where they served as a source of spiritual teachings and wisdom.

During the Khmer rule in the Angkor Empire (9th to 15th centuries), literary production flourished, with the famous inscriptions on stone tablets on the temples of Angkor bearing witness to this period. These inscriptions included mythological tales, historical accounts, and royal decrees documenting the cultural and political life of the era.

During the colonial era under French rule (1863-1953), Cambodian literature underwent a transformation as Western literary forms and ideas were introduced. Cambodian writers began to publish their works in the Khmer language, which contributed to the formation of a modern literary identity that combined traditional and modern elements.

After independence from France in 1953, Cambodian literature continued to develop, with writers such as Nhok Them and U Sam Oeur making significant contributions. Literature increasingly focused on social issues, political issues, and reflection on Cambodian identity in a changing world.

During the Khmer Rouge period (1975-1979), cultural production was severely suppressed, and many writers and intellectuals were persecuted or killed. This led to a drastic decline in literary production and a loss of significant works and talent.

Since the 1990s, however, Cambodian literature has been experiencing a resurgence, supported by initiatives to promote the Khmer script and train a new generation of writers and poets. Modern Cambodian writers such as Soth Polin, Kho Tararith, and Loung Ung have gained international recognition and contribute to the advancement of Khmer literature by addressing contemporary issues and cultural challenges.

Cambodian literature remains a living expression of the country's cultural identity and history, reflecting both past and present, bridging tradition and modernity. It is an important part of Cambodia's cultural heritage and contributes to global literary diversity.

Musical Traditions: Sounds of the Old Kingdom

Cambodia's musical traditions go deep into the history of the ancient kingdom and reflect a rich cultural diversity that has grown over centuries. One of the most distinctive forms of music is classical Cambodian court music, which is closely linked to the royal tradition and plays a significant role in the cultural life of the country. This music is often accompanied by traditional instruments such as the roneat (a type of xylophone), the sralai (a bamboo flute), and the tro (a plucked lute).

Another important element of the Cambodian musical tradition is the court dances, which are closely linked to classical music and often depict religious and mythological stories. These dances, like the Apsara dance, are known for their graceful movements and complex hand gestures that require a high level of artistic training.

Cambodia's traditional music also includes folk music, which is played in different regions of the country and is often heard at festivals and celebrations. Typical instruments in Cambodian folk music are the tro khmer (a simple long-necked lute), the chhing (a kind of cymbal) and the skor (drum).

During the Khmer Rouge era in the late 1970s, Cambodian music was severely suppressed, and many musicians and artists were persecuted or killed. This led to a loss of knowledge and traditional skills, which greatly influenced the country's musical landscape.

Since the 1990s, however, the Cambodian music scene has been undergoing a renewal, supported by efforts to preserve and revitalize traditional music forms. Modern musicians and composers, such as Meas Samoun and Chinary Ung, have helped to combine traditional elements with contemporary influences, fostering a dynamic and eclectic music scene.

The sounds of the ancient kingdom remain an important part of Cambodia's cultural identity and serve as a source of inspiration and recreation for the country's people. They contribute to the preservation of cultural heritage while providing a platform for creative innovation and expression.

Dance and theatre: performances and performance venues

Dance and theatre play a central role in Cambodian culture, offering insight into the country's rich history and traditions. Traditional Cambodian dance is closely associated with religious rites and royal festivals. One of the most well-known forms of dance is the Apsara dance, which includes elegant movements and complex hand gestures that depict mythological stories and historical events. This dance form is an integral part of Cambodia's cultural identity and is often performed in temples and at royal ceremonies.

In addition to the Apsara dance, there are also other traditional dances such as the Robam Trot (flirtatious dance form), the Robam Choun Por (dance of the royal palace guard) and the Robam Tep Apsara (dance of the heavenly nymphs). Each of these dances has its own unique movements and musical accompaniments, showing a deep connection to the country's history and customs.

The traditional Cambodian theater, known as Lakhon Bassac or Lakhon Khol, integrates music, dance, and acting. These forms of theatre are often mythological or historically inspired and have been cultivated for centuries to portray stories from the Ramayana epic and other classic works. Performances typically take place in pavilions or on special stages, which are often ornately decorated with traditional motifs.

In recent decades, the Cambodian dance and theatre scene has evolved, with modern interpretations of traditional forms taking place alongside contemporary works. The country's artists are committed to preserving its rich cultural heritage while exploring new forms of expression that reflect the diversity and vibrancy of Cambodian culture.

Travel tips and practical information for visitors

For visitors who want to explore Cambodia, there are some essential travel tips and practical information that can help make the trip enjoyable and enriching. First of all, it is important to be clear about the best time to visit. Cambodia has a tropical climate with two main seasons: a rainy season from May to October and a dry season from November to April. The cooler dry season is often recommended as the best time to visit, especially for visits to the temples of Angkor and other historical sites, as temperatures are more pleasant and rain is rare.

To enter Cambodia, most visitors will need a visa, which can be applied for either upon arrival at the airport or online in advance. It is advisable to find out in advance about the current entry requirements and make sure that all the necessary documents are available.

In terms of accommodation, Cambodia offers a variety of options, from luxury resorts to budget hostels. Popular tourist destinations such as Siem Reap and Phnom Penh have a wide range of accommodations, while more remote regions can offer more basic guesthouses and boutique hotels. Early booking is recommended, especially in high season, to ensure the best selection and prices.

There are several options available for getting around the country. Tuk-tuks are a frequently used and characteristic form of transport in cities and for short distances between attractions. In larger cities such as Phnom Penh and Siem Reap, there are also taxis and motorcycle taxis (motodops), which offer a convenient way to get around. For longer distances within the country, buses and minivans are available, which have regular connections between the cities and tourist destinations.

In terms of health, it is advisable to check the necessary vaccinations before the trip and refresh them if necessary. Malaria is present in some rural areas, so it is recommended to take appropriate precautions and use mosquito repellents. Drinking water should always be obtained from sealed bottles to avoid stomach problems.

Culturally, it is important to respect local etiquette and wear appropriate clothing, especially when visiting religious sites such as temples. Visitors are expected to remove their shoes and behave respectfully when entering such sacred places.

Finally, Cambodia is a fascinating country with a rich history, breathtaking nature and a warm hospitality of its people. With the right preparations and an open mind, visitors can have unforgettable experiences and discover a variety of sights and cultural treasures.

Closing remarks

The final word of a book about Cambodia is intended to encourage readers to deepen their understanding and appreciation of this fascinating country. Cambodia, rich in thousands of years of history and a multifaceted culture, has experienced numerous ups and downs over the centuries. From the majestic temples of Angkor to the vibrant cities of Phnom Penh and Siem Reap, the country offers a variety of sights and experiences that attract both historians and adventurers alike.

The preservation of Cambodian culture and heritage is crucial for the future of the country. Traditional festivals and customs such as the Khmer New Year (Chaul Chnam Thmey) or the Water Festival (Bon Om Touk) reflect not only people's joy and sense of community, but also their deep-rooted spiritual beliefs.

Cambodians are known for their hospitality and warmth, which never ceases to impress visitors from all over the world. The local cuisine, characterized by fresh ingredients such as rice, fish and tropical fruits, is a culinary experience in itself and offers an insight into the diversity and variety of flavors of the region.

Over the past few decades, Cambodia has become a popular tourist destination that attracts both adventurers and recreationists. The development of the tourism sector has created new opportunities, but it also poses challenges in terms of environmental protection and sustainable development. Preserving the country's natural beauty and protecting wildlife are at the heart of efforts to preserve Cambodia for generations to come.

Finally, this book invites you to explore Cambodia with open eyes and an open heart. Every visit to this country offers the opportunity to experience history, enjoy the beauty of nature and experience the warm hospitality of its inhabitants. May this journey through the pages of this book be just the beginning of deeper insights and a lasting connection to this unique and unforgettable country.